# SERENDIPITY

# LEADER'S HANDBOOK

*FOR*

# SMALL GROUPS

SERENDIPITY SMALL GROUP RESOURCES

**Executive Editor**
Lyman Coleman

**Project Editor**
Steve Sheely

**Assistant Editor**
Timothy Hedrick

**Contributors**
Neal McBride
Marty Scales
Gary Treichler
Stan Geyer
Thom Corrigan
Mickey Elliot

**Cartoons**
Robert Shull

**Typesetting**
Sharon Penington

**Graphics Design**
Erika Tiepel
Maurice Lydick

SERENDIPITY / Box 1012 / Littleton, CO 80160 / 1-800-525-9563
© 1994 Serendipity House. All rights reserved.

95 96 97 98 / CHG / 5 4 3 2

# Welcome to Your Small Group Adventure!

You are preparing to embark on a wonderful journey. Leading a small group can be one of the most rewarding, life-changing, and challenging experiences in your life. There are few things more satisfying than bringing a group of people together in Jesus' name, and learning how to love one another.

This Small Group *Leader's Handbook* contains everything you need to begin your own small group. All the important fundamentals of successful small group leadership are included in these pages. If you are nervous about leading a small group, don't worry! By the time you complete the six sessions in this manual, you will feel ready and excited about leading a small group.

This manual is meant to be used with the *Director's Workbook,* from the *Serendipity Small Group Starter Kit.* The director of your small group program has worked very hard in preparation for your training. Your small group leader training has been custom-designed to fit the unique needs of your church!

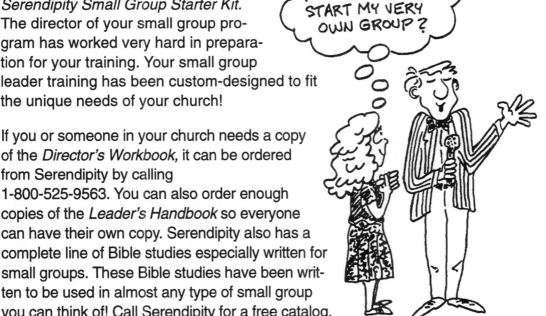

If you or someone in your church needs a copy of the *Director's Workbook,* it can be ordered from Serendipity by calling 1-800-525-9563. You can also order enough copies of the *Leader's Handbook* so everyone can have their own copy. Serendipity also has a complete line of Bible studies especially written for small groups. These Bible studies have been written to be used in almost any type of small group you can think of! Call Serendipity for a free catalog.

May God bless your efforts to lead a small group! May his blessings abound as you strive to bring people to Christ in an acceptance place to grow and heal.

# Table Of Contents

**Page**

Session 1................................................................................6
- Why have small groups?.................................................7
- What is our church's mission?.......................................8
- What is a small group.....................................................9
- What is our small group dream?...................................10
- Self-Quiz #1...................................................................12

Session 2..............................................................................15
- What does a small group leader do?............................16
- What is the 3-legged stool?..........................................18
- What happens during a small group meeting?............19
- What is a group covenant?............................................20
- Self-Quiz #2...................................................................22

Session 3..............................................................................24
- What is good communication?......................................25
- The small group stairway?............................................28
- How do you choose material for your small group?....29
- How does a group choose a ministry project?............32
- Self-Quiz #3...................................................................33

Session 4..............................................................................35
- What is a healthy small group?.....................................36
- What if there is a problem?............................................37
- Can small groups have fun, too?..................................39
- Self-Quiz #4...................................................................40

Session 5 . . . . . . . . . . . . . . . . . . . . . . . . . . . . . . . . . . . . . . . . . . . . . . . . . . . 42
   • Can a small group "grow up"? . . . . . . . . . . . . . . . . . . . . . . . . . . . . . . . . . 43
   • How long does community take? . . . . . . . . . . . . . . . . . . . . . . . . . . . . . . . 44
   • When can a small group leader "step back"? . . . . . . . . . . . . . . . . . . . . . 45
   • Should groups always be open to new people? . . . . . . . . . . . . . . . . . . . . 46
   • What is our strategy for multiplying groups? . . . . . . . . . . . . . . . . . . . . . 48
   • Self-Quiz #5 . . . . . . . . . . . . . . . . . . . . . . . . . . . . . . . . . . . . . . . . . . . . . 49

Session 6 . . . . . . . . . . . . . . . . . . . . . . . . . . . . . . . . . . . . . . . . . . . . . . . . . . . 51
   • What kind of people join a small group? . . . . . . . . . . . . . . . . . . . . . . . . . 52
   • How do I start a group? . . . . . . . . . . . . . . . . . . . . . . . . . . . . . . . . . . . . . 53
   • How does a small group end? . . . . . . . . . . . . . . . . . . . . . . . . . . . . . . . . 55
   • What is on our small group calendar? . . . . . . . . . . . . . . . . . . . . . . . . . . 57
   • Where can a leader get support? . . . . . . . . . . . . . . . . . . . . . . . . . . . . . . 58
   • Self-Quiz #6 . . . . . . . . . . . . . . . . . . . . . . . . . . . . . . . . . . . . . . . . . . . . . 60

# Session 1

**Let's get started with the basics:**

- Why have small groups? ........................................ 7

- What is our church's mission? .................................. 8

- What is a small group? ......................................... 9

- What is our small group dream? ................................ 10

- Self-Quiz #1 .................................................. 12

# *Why Have Small Groups?*

A small group program involves a lot of hard work. But the rewards are tremendous! The questions about small groups below are meant to be answered after you have watched the video, "Building Quality Into Life."

Tim Hedrick and the folks at the Community Church of Joy in Phoenix, Arizona, produced this video. This is a Lutheran Church that has developed an effective small group program based on the principles taught for years by Serendipity.

After you have watched the video discuss the following questions:

1. Several people in the video describe their small group meeting format. Have you ever been in a small group? What was the format of your meeting?

2. The people in the video came from several different types of small groups. What types of small groups have you been a part of?

3. Do the people in the small groups seem friendly? Or are they threatening? Do they seem authentic? Would you enjoy being in a small group with the people in the video?

4. The small group members in this video describe profound improvements in their quality of life. How do you think a small group can do that?

5. How could small groups "Build Quality Into Life" in the life of your church?

6. What are some of your reservations about small groups?

# *What Is Our Church's Mission?*

Every church has a mission. Write your church mission statement in the box below:

Our church exists to . . .




Our church is committed to . . .




Our mission is . . .



• How do you think small groups can fulfill this mission statement?

# *What Is a Small Group?*

Sure, it's a little group of people! Let's define what a small group is at your church. Write the definition of a small group in the box below:

<br><br><br><br><br><br><br><br><br><br>

• How is this definition different than what you expected?

• Have you been in a small group before? Is it similar to the above definition? Why or why not?

# *What Is Our Small Group Dream?*

Your church leaders, including your small group director, have worked hard to formulate your small group vision. By sharing in this vision, you can help promote the dream. As a trained small group leader, you can be an ambassador for small groups in your church. Record the details of your church's small group dream:

What types of groups are we going to have?

**Relationship Groups**
❑ Assimilation groups
❑ Affinity groups
❑ Recreational groups

**Need-Based Groups**
❑ Enrichment groups
❑ Support groups
❑ Recovery groups
❑ Shame-based groups

**Discipleship Groups**
❑ Bible study groups
❑ Christian skills groups
❑ Topical study groups
❑ Growth groups
❑ Accountability groups
❑ Sermon discussion groups
❑ Prayer groups
❑ Graduation groups

**Ministry Groups**
❑ Service groups
❑ Policy setting groups
❑ Administrative groups
❑ Skill development groups
❑ Outreach groups

How many groups is our church going to start? Which types of groups is your church going to start?

What is the difference between the different types of groups our church is going to start?

What benefits will our church receive from small groups?

- ❑ it's a way for people to get to know each other
- ❑ they encourage a sense of community in our church
- ❑ they give people an opportunity for in-depth Bible study
- ❑ it's a place where people can really care for one another
- ❑ it's an effective way to encourage spiritual growth
- ❑ it's a place where hurting people can go for healing
- ❑ it's a place to develop spiritual leadership
- ❑ other:_____

What needs can small groups meet in our church?

- ❑ **Pastoral care:** it's where real empathy can take place
- ❑ **Discipleship:** it's where spiritual discipline can be fostered by supporting each other and holding each other accountable
- ❑ **Compassion:** it's where "broken people" can gather and attend to each other's wounds
- ❑ **Edification:** it's the chief means by which new believers can grow into spiritual maturity
- ❑ **Mobilization:** it's the staging area in which people are best equipped and released for ministry in their world
- ❑ **Socialization:** it's where people can make friends and feel a sense of family

According to the small group dream, what will the small group program look like after one year?

After five years?

How will your church's small group program fit into your church's mission statement?

# Self-Quiz #1

Each session ends with a self-quiz. Complete each self-quiz before your next meeting. Each self-quiz has four parts: Bible Study, Reflection, Preparation, Prayer.

 **Bible Study:** The Bible contains a wealth of information about small groups.

The Old Testament. Evidence of corporate life is common in the Old Testament, including the very nature of God. The creation story uses the term "Elohim" to describe God. "Elohim" is a plural term, indicating the triune nature of God. We use the term "Trinity" to describe the relationship between the Father, Son and Holy Spirit. Some have said that God exists in a "small group." The very nature of God is relational.

Group involvement was also very important in the Old Testament. There is no doubt that belonging to a group was critical to God's plan for his people. God has never expected his children to have a relationship with him in isolation. From God's perspective, a relationship with him should always thrive in some sort of community with other believers.

Fill in the blanks below by naming the different groups an Israelite belonged to:

_____ - Deuteronomy 6:6. The Israelites were a chosen people/group, set apart by God from all other people on the face of the earth.

_____ - Genesis 49. The house of Israel, by virtue of its descent from the twelve sons of Jacob, was divided into 12 sub-groups.

_____ - Numbers 4:21-22. Tribes were further broken down into groups of extended relatives, resulting in 57 clans.

_____ - Genesis 50:8. Literally "house," the various clans were divided down into family sub-groups, several generations of relatives living in the same dwelling, including servants.

_____ - As a patriarchal system, the immediate family including a husband, wife and children were the smallest group within the Jewish identity; e.g., "son of. . ." The family was the heart of Jewish society.

The entire legal and religious system of Judaism was dependent upon these groups, and a corporate understanding of faith and behavior. Worship, faith and the law were based upon a lifestyle of belonging to these different groups. Devotion to God was not an individual effort.

**Reflection:** These questions give you a chance to reflect back on what you learned in Session 1. You might be asked to share your answers at the next session.

1. Small groups can meet many needs in life. What are the most pressing needs in your life? (relationships, family issues, gaining control, stress, spiritual growth, making new friends, plugging into the church, etc.)

2. What has been your personal small group experience? What type of group was it? When? Where? What did you like about it?

3. Which type of small group would you be most interested in leading?

**Preparation:** Get ready for Session 2 by answering the following questions:

1. To get an idea about the importance of group building, ask yourself the following questions:

&#10065; yes &#10065; no   Do you typically take a while to "warm up" before you can talk comfortably about the important issues in your life?

&#10065; yes &#10065; no   Would it feel awkward to kick off a brand new small group by asking, "How can we pray about your spiritual life?"

&#10065; yes &#10065; no   Do you think it would be strange to turn and walk away from someone after they spoke honestly about an issue in their life?

2. What components do you think a small group meeting should include?

&#10065; a bunch of tasty snacks
&#10065; juggling
&#10065; accordion music
&#10065; snake handling
&#10065; arm-wrestling

**Prayer:** Before your next meeting, pray about the following . . .

• asking God to bless your training sessions
• that your desire to be a group leader will glorify God
• that small groups will assist your church in its mission

# Session 2

Session #2 covers the following topics:

- **What does a small group leader do?** . . . . . . . . . . . . . . . . . . . . . . . . . . . . . . . . . **16**

- **What is the 3-legged stool?** . . . . . . . . . . . . . . . . . . . . . . . . . . . . . . . . . . . . . . . . 18

- **What happens during a small group meeting?** . . . . . . . . . . . . . . . . . . . . . . . . . 19

- **What is a group covenant?** . . . . . . . . . . . . . . . . . . . . . . . . . . . . . . . . . . . . . . . . . 20

- **Self-quiz #2** . . . . . . . . . . . . . . . . . . . . . . . . . . . . . . . . . . . . . . . . . . . . . . . . . . . . . 22

# What Does a Small Group Leader Do?

**Leadership Skills for a Group Leader**

Here is a list of the **skills** small group leaders need. Your small group program will require certain skills. Mark the skills you will need to be a small group leader:

**required**    **recommended**

| required | recommended | |
|---|---|---|
| ❑ | ❑ | They are good listeners |
| ❑ | ❑ | They are not afraid of confrontation |
| ❑ | ❑ | They are good problem solvers |
| ❑ | ❑ | They possess good social skills |
| ❑ | ❑ | They are able to recognize abuse |
| ❑ | ❑ | They can effectively share the gospel |
| ❑ | ❑ | They manage their time well |
| ❑ | ❑ | They are able to affirm others |
| ❑ | ❑ | They have a nurturing spirit |
| ❑ | ❑ | Their lives exemplify spiritual disciplines |
| ❑ | ❑ | They have skills in administration |
| ❑ | ❑ | They can explain the small group vision |
| ❑ | ❑ | They can teach about prayer |
| ❑ | ❑ | They know how to run a meeting |
| ❑ | ❑ | They know how to facilitate sharing |
| ❑ | ❑ | They have basic counseling skills |
| ❑ | ❑ | They can make referrals when needed |
| ❑ | ❑ | They are able to keep a confidence |
| ❑ | ❑ | They have basic Bible knowledge |
| ❑ | ❑ | They know how to multiply a group |
| ❑ | ❑ | They can make contacts with new prospects |
| ❑ | ❑ | They know how to welcome new members |
| ❑ | ❑ | They are able to lead worship and music |
| ❑ | ❑ | They understand the group process |
| ❑ | ❑ | They are able to identify spiritual gifts |
| ❑ | ❑ | They know how to ask for assistance |
| ❑ | ❑ | They can evaluate group progress |

## Responsibilities of a Group Leader

Let's do the same thing for the **specific responsibilities** for small group leaders. Again, mark those responsibilities that are expected of a small group leader.

❏ Invite prospective group members to attend the meeting.

❏ Convene the group at your regularly scheduled frequency.

❏ Follow up members and prospective members with personal visits, phone calls and correspondence.

❏ Prepare an agenda to include an Ice-Breaker, Bible study, sharing and prayer, or follow the material that uses this format.

❏ Pray for each group member in preparation for your next meeting.

❏ Notify the pastoral staff of any acute condition requiring special attention.

❏ Take advantage of any additional training opportunities as they come available.

❏ Create by example and leadership an environment where each group member feels accepted, cared for and loved.

❏ Guide the group to agree on a covenant which will include the purpose and goals of the group, meeting arrangements and ground rules.

❏ Delegate to individual members of the group such responsibilities as hosting, leading music, planning refreshments and social activities, and occasionally leading portions of the meeting.

❏ Encourage regular church attendance by each member.

❏ Complete and submit all the required reports to your coach or the small group director when they are due.

❏ Submit any orders for curriculum to your coach or small group director and collect money from the group members.

❏ Select and develop an apprentice for your group. Mentor them and help them acquire leadership skills. Encourage their attendance at leader training sessions.

❏ Provide opportunities for the apprentice to lead the group in your presence **and** in your absence (at your discretion).

# *What Is the 3-Legged Stool?*

The 3-legged stool signifies the three components every small group needs to stay balanced.

A small group needs to be balanced, resting evenly on three components: Bible Study, Group Building and Mission.

**Bible Study:** Studying and discussing the scripture is an important part of any small group meeting—every group needs a source of inspiration. However, no stool can stand on one leg! Bible study by itself can become boring and top-heavy, leading to spiritual indigestion. This is the "school" part of the meeting.

**Group Building:** The process of "becoming" a group and caring for one another—like they did in the Upper Room—takes time, effort and communication. Unless a group is committed to this and works at it, the group will probably fail. Again, if a group focuses exclusively on group building (like some support groups today), it can become co-dependent, cliquish, and morbidly introspective. The group-building part of the meeting is the "hospital."

**Mission:** Reaching out to others is a good way to keep a group from becoming too ingrown. A small group is a tremendous opportunity for people to use their closeness to share Christ's love with others. Alcoholics Anonymous really pushes the 12th Step: "Having had a spiritual awakening as the result of these steps we tried to carry this message to alcoholics and to practice these principles in all our affairs." Again, if a small group tries to rest solely on the leg of mission or task, it can lead to unfulfillment and burn out. Mission is the "army" aspect of a small group.

# *What Happens During a Small Group Meeting?*

Here is a very simple format for a small group meeting, but notice how group building times are included in the meeting:

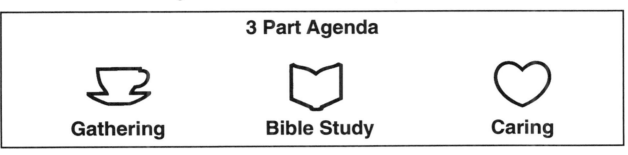

## 3 Part Agenda

| Gathering | Bible Study | Caring |

**Gathering (15 minutes)**
This is the time to "unwind," enjoy some refreshments and begin the meeting with an "Ice-Breaker." An Ice-Breaker is a valuable tool to get a group smiling and laughing, and help them begin thinking and talking about their lives. Ice-Breakers open doors of communication among a group, inviting memories, dreams and personal information into the group.

**Bible Study (30-45 minutes)**
This is the time for "head-to-head" communication of Bible study and discussion. The group begins by discussing the passage, and then they can break into sub-groups of four so everyone will have more time to talk. Then the group gets back together, the Bible study is completed, and a few more minutes is used to discuss group business and the ministry project.

**Caring (30-45 minutes)**
This is the time for "Heart-Warmers." Heart-Warmers help a group pray about their lives, apply the Bible study, and share affirmation with other group members. The caring time is "heart-to-heart" communication and it is the most important time in the meeting.

Here is a list of all the different components which can be included in a small group meeting. Check those activities which your small group director has chosen:

- ❑ Ice-Breaker
- ❑ Review of group covenant
- ❑ Introduction to Bible story
- ❑ Bible discussion in foursomes
- ❑ Worship: singing and praise
- ❑ Discussion of group's ministry project
- ❑ Fellowship
- ❑ Discussion of upcoming group activities
- ❑ Accountability exercise
- ❑ Prayer for one another
- ❑ Discussion of prospective group members

- ❑ Welcoming of new members
- ❑ Opening prayer
- ❑ Group discussion of Bible story
- ❑ Reports on answered prayer
- ❑ Prayer to apply Bible study
- ❑ Prayer for group's ministry project
- ❑ Prayer for prospective group members
- ❑ Group affirmation
- ❑ Sharing of prayer requests
- ❑ Prayer for the church
- ❑ Tasty refreshments

# *What is a Group Covenant?*

What is a Group Covenant? The group covenant form is a tremendous way for a small group to get together and agree on the basic details of the group. This way, everyone knows what is going on, and everyone has the opportunity to toss in their "two cents" regarding how the group is run.

Here is a basic group covenant. Your small group director has copies of this covenant for you to use. Some of the issues on this covenant may have already been decided by your small group director.

1. The purpose of our group is. . .

2. Our goals will be. . .

3. We will meet for _____ weeks, after which we will decide if we wish to continue as a group. If we do decide to continue, we will also reconsider this covenant.

4. We will meet on _____ from _____ to _____ and we will strive to start on time and end on time.

   • Refreshments will be taken care of by . . .
   • Childcare will be handled by. . .
   • Bible study material will be. . .

5. We will meet at _____or we will rotate from house to house.

6. We will agree to the following ground rules for our small group:

   ❑ **Priority:** While we are in this small group, we will give group meetings priority.
   ❑ **Participation:** Everyone is given the right to their own opinion and "dumb questions" are respected. Dominating the discussion is discouraged.
   ❑ **Confidentiality:** Anything that is said in the meeting is never repeated outside the meeting.
   ❑ **Empty Chair:** The group stays open to new people as long as group size and space requirements allow. However, the group might wish to close halfway through the covenant, but remain open during the first half.
   ❑ **Support:** Permission is given to call upon each other in time of need—even in the middle of the night.
   ❑ **Ministry Project:** We will try and choose, plan, and complete a ministry project to assist one another, our church, or our community.
   ❑ **Other:**

## Ground rules

Certain ground rules for your small groups are a good idea. Here is a listing of ground rules you could add to your group covenant.

❑ **Priority:** *"While we are in this small group, we will give group meetings priority."* Consistency and dependability are crucial for developing an atmosphere of trust. If a group member is dissatisfied or frustrated with the progress of the group, everyone should be open to corrections or changes. If someone cannot attend a meeting, they should call the group leader and notify them of their absence.

❑ **Participation:** *"Everyone is given the right to their own opinion and "dumb questions" are respected. Dominating the discussion is discouraged."* It needs to be stressed that you don't have to be a Bible scholar or have a religious background to participate in a small group. The group might need to be encouraged to help everyone feel accepted, whatever their background.

❑ **Confidentiality:** *"Anything said in this meeting is never repeated outside the meeting."* Sometimes things are shared in small group settings which should not be discussed outside of the group setting. Developing an atmosphere of trust and security is an important process of small groups. If something awkward or inappropriate is said during a meeting, the group should be reminded of the confidentiality policy. The only time this policy should be disregarded is when someone threatens to hurt themselves or someone else, but that person should be told that the confidentiality policy must be broken for their protection.

❑ **Empty Chair:** *"The group stays open to new people as long as group size and space requirements allow. However, the group might wish to remain open through the first half of their covenant, and closed to new members during the second half."* Of course, outreach is an important function of small groups. Visitors can discover a sense of acceptance and belonging that can be missed in a large worship service. However, care must be taken when guests are invited who have no previous experience with small groups, or guests who have no intention of joining the group.

❑ **Support:** *"Permission is given to call upon each other in time of need—even in the middle of the night."* Being available for one another is an exciting part of the friendships which can be built in a small group. However, it takes time to develop these kinds of relationships. It is always nice to say, "Why don't you call me if you need someone to talk to this week?" Or ask, "Would it be all right if we talked?"

❑ **Ministry Project:** *"We will try and choose, plan, and complete a ministry project to assist our church or our community."* A group can make a commitment in their covenant to work to set up a ministry project. This is an important decision because of the ministry a group can do and the team building which can occur among the group members.

# *Self-Quiz #2*

**Bible Study:** The Bible contains a wealth of information about small groups.

The New Testament portrays Jesus as a small group leader. Jesus spent the majority of his time with his small group, the 12 disciples (Luke 6:13), and he chose to minister in the framework of intimate relationships.

There are other important features to Jesus' involvement with his small group:

• Jesus involved himself in large group **and** small group ministry (Mark 12:37).

• Jesus' small group consumed the majority of his time. Jesus was with his disciples constantly: they traveled together, ate together, lived together, and experienced hardships together. As the crucifixion drew near, Jesus spent more and more time with his small group.

• Relationships were more important to Jesus than religious organizations. Jesus' primary concern was the salvation of people, not the establishment of a religious institution. He spent his time caring for, healing, listening, forgiving, encouraging, and teaching people. The **only** organization Jesus spent time with was his small group.

• The small group was Jesus' primary context to teach and exemplify spiritual knowledge and behavior. Jesus and his disciples was a living/learning laboratory.

• The primary method Jesus used to train leaders was the small group. The men in Jesus' small group literally changed the world.

What can happen in someone's Christian life in a small group that cannot happen without small group involvement?

**Reflection:** These questions give you a chance to reflect back on what you learned in Session 2. You might be asked to share your answers at the next session.

1. How do you feel about the skills and responsibilities required of small group leaders? How do you think you will feel after your training has been completed?

2. What do you think a small group meeting would be like if it began immediately with Bible study and did not have a time of "gathering" with an Ice-Breaker?

3. Similarly, what do you think a small group meeting would be like if it did not end with a time of caring, neglecting Heart-Warmers such as prayer and affirmation?

4. What components of the meeting agenda are you uncomfortable or unfamiliar with?

5. How comfortable do you feel about praying out loud?

6. How do you think someone might feel if they were expected to pray out loud for the first time in their new small group meeting?

7. Which of the ground rules would you like to see in the group you lead?

**Preparation:** Get ready for Session 3 by answering the following questions:

1. When are you more likely to speak in clichés?

2. When are you more likely to "open up" in a conversation?

3. How would you encourage a group of people to "open up" with one another?

4. Have you ever been a part of a church group that had a ministry project in addition to its main function?

**Prayer:** Before your next meeting, pray about the following:

Return to the list of skills a small group leader needs. You might feel unsure about some of the skills you need in order to lead a group properly. For those skills that are new to you, pray that God will help you develop the necessary skills.

# Session 3

**In Session #3 we will cover:**

• **What is good communication?**.....................................25

• **The small group stairway?**.......................................28

• **How do you choose material for your small group?**....................29

• **How does a group choose a ministry project?**........................32

• **Self-quiz #3.**...................................................33

# *What Is Good Communication?*

"Blah, blah, blah." Yeah, sure, everyone knows how to talk, but does everyone know how to *communicate?* Communication is a skill especially important for your leaders.

Let's take a look at the different levels of communication. This list was developed by Roberta Hestenes.

**Level 1:** _____ This type of communication is very safe. Topics include the weather, family and current affairs. We use words and phrases like, "How are you?," "I like your shirt," and "Boy, it sure is hot." Each person remains comfortably behind the screen, and no personal disclosure takes place.

**Level 2:** _____ In level two we talk about actual events, facts and basic information, but not about ourselves. We might talk about what is going on in people's lives, but not talk about our own. We might say, "At our small group planning meeting we decided to develop three support groups."

**Level 3:** _____ This is where some real communication begins. We begin to take some risks by expressing some of our own ideas and opinions. We might say, "I think people who are racist don't know how to deal with their own fear and anger."

**Level 4:** _____ At this level we offer our feelings about facts, ideas and opinions. This is a move beyond the sharing of thoughts into the realm of emotions. This is risky because when we are emotional, we are more vulnerable. An example of level four communication would be, "When I talk to people I assume they will disagree with me. I feel like people don't like me."

**Level 5:** _____This is "peak" communication, a time of the deepest level of openness, transparency and self-disclosure. Level five communication are the things that people typically keep hidden. Shame plays a big part in keeping many people away from communication of this kind. Here is an example: "John and I have really been depressed and discouraged. Sally came into our room Tuesday night and told us she is pregnant. I feel so angry and helpless. . . I don't know what to do."

Recognizing the five levels of communication can help a small group leader guide a group toward deeper levels of communication. However, there are certain skills which can encourage this valuable process.

Here is a list of communication skills that any small group leader can use to make their group a place of deeper levels of communication. You will notice that these skills show the leader as a facilitator more than a lecturer. Robert Bolton's book *People Skills,* required reading for small group leaders in some programs, is a valuable resource in developing communication skills.

**Affirmation.** By receiving all statements warmly, encouraging honest responses, etc.—a small group leader can help the group feel more comfortable with deeper levels of communication. Affirmation must be the heartbeat of every Christian small group.

**Confrontation.** When done with love **and** honesty, confrontation can be a wonderful experience. There was a time when it was common— even in Christian groups—to practice confrontation on each other in the group. If you shared, you might be confronted about the issue or feelings you shared. If you didn't share, you would be confronted about not being open with the group.

**Inviting.** The extroverts in a group will have little trouble "chiming in" when they have something to say. The introverts, however, might need a little nudge. Inviting is a communication skill which encourages the quieter people to share their thoughts and feelings. Usually it can be done simply: "Joey. . .?" or "Mary Ellen, what do you think?"

Extending is similar to inviting, extending encourages a person to continue talking about something. Extending can be done with a simple, "And. . .?" or "Go on." Another extending phrase is, "tell us more about what you mean by that."

**Active Listening.** When someone can see that they are being listened to they are more likely to communicate more openly. Active listening skills include making eye contact, an attentive posture, and nodding occasionally.

**Summarizing.** This is a valuable skill that is easy to do. Periodically, the leader summarizes what someone has said. It helps a person know that they are being listened to when someone is able to accurately paraphrase their remarks. Example: "It sounds like your relationship with your children is frustrating to you."

**Border Patrol.** Sometimes good communication skills involve protecting the group from improper communication. This usually involves controlling statements that impose on someone's personal boundaries. Advice-giving is an example of this. The task of a group is to listen empathetically and provide support, not tell someone how to live their life. "You" statements, instead of "I" statements also require the action of a leader to step in.

**Rescuing.** When a group begins to achieve Level 4 and 5 communication, the leader needs to be prepared. Let's say Bob shares a struggle in his life and the leader is not sure how deep a hurt this is for Bob. A key act he should take is to affirm Bob's words, "Thanks for sharing that" is always a key phrase. The leader then goes on to ask, "Are you okay, now?" Bob responds, "The truth is, I'm running on empty. I don't see any way out." At this point, the leader had better come through, because Bob has taken his shirt off. He's dying right in front of the group. The leader needs to make sure that Bob is given every opportunity and encouragement to open up and share, and to have his sharing heard and affirmed. Bob doesn't need advice. He doesn't need to have his problems fixed. He just needs friends who will listen and care. Rescuing means being there in a supportive way when someone lets their guard down.

# The Small Group Stairway

Have you ever used a stair-climbing machine? It seems like you will never get to the top! A small group, however, has a "top floor." The top floor of a small group is a time of trusting, loving fellowship usually highlighted by prayer for one another. This is a time of community, when the Holy Spirit can do remarkable things in the life of your group.

This time of community does not happen automatically. A group needs to be guided in a way that beckons people to this period of intimacy and openness. That is the reasoning behind the "Small Group Stairway."

 A Heart-Warmer fulfills the last step. This is a time of sharing and prayer, a time of affirmation and accountability. If the meeting format has gradually moved up the stairway, this portion of the meeting can be life-changing

 The fourth step involves the discussion of group business. During this time the group can discuss their group covenant, plan a ministry project or discuss who they would like to bring to the group. These items can be prayed about during the last step.

 The third step is personalizing the Bible study. Instead of "How did David handle his relationship with his brother?" the question becomes, "How do I handle the relationships with **my** family?"

 The second step begins Bible study and discussion. This portion of the Bible study focuses on the content—what does it say? This is a chance for group members to respond to what the passage really means.

 The group begins with an Ice-Breaker, which gives the group permission to laugh and talk about themselves.

# How Do You Choose Material for Your Small Group?

The destination of a small group is spiritual growth, healing, and service—all within the power of community. If your destination is community, you need the right map to get you there.

The best Bible study material for groups is written with a sensitivity to the group process. Some material you can use in a small group includes Ice-Breakers and Heart-Warmers. That is, it recognizes the importance of helping a group get started properly, and they also include ways to help a group close in prayer or affirmation.

Here are some useful principles for the type of Bible study most effective in a small group:

1. **Group vs. Personal Bible Study:** Group Bible study is different from private study, especially at the beginning. Group Bible study helps a group become a community by giving everyone the opportunity to share their spiritual history.

2. **Gradual Disclosure:** Sharing your spiritual story with anybody is scary (especially with people you do not know). However, it is easier if you can start off by talking about somebody else's spiritual story first, such as the story of a character in the Bible. This makes it easier to discuss our own stories as we compare them to the story in scripture. This is called moving across the "disclosure scale." Start with low risk by asking the question about how Peter met God and then move to higher risk by asking "How did I meet God?"

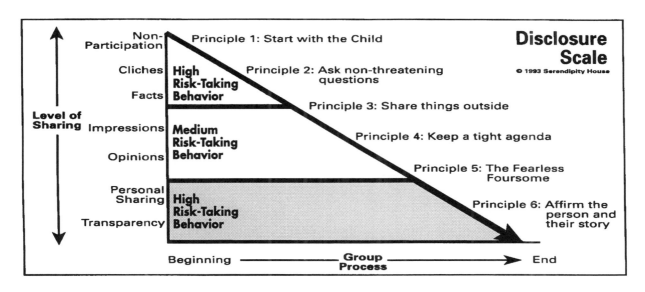

3. **Open Questions/Right Brain:** Open-ended questions are better than closed questions. Open questions allow for options, observations, and a variety of opinions in which no one is right or wrong. Similarly, "right-brained" questions are better than "left-brained" questions. Right-brained questions seek out your first impressions, tone, motives and subjective feelings about the text. Right-brained questions work well with narratives.

4. **Multiple Choice Options:** Multiple choice questionnaires encourage people who know very little about the Bible. Given a set of multiple choice options, a new believer is not threatened, and a shy person is not intimidated. Everyone has something to contribute.

5. **Tight Agenda:** A tight agenda is better than a loose agenda for beginning small groups. Those people who might be nervous about "sharing" will find comfort knowing that the meeting agenda has been carefully organized. The more structure the first few meetings have the better, especially for a new group.

   Some people are afraid that a structured agenda will limit discussion. In fact, the opposite is true. The Serendipity agenda is designed to keep the discussion focused on what's important and to bring out genuine feelings, issues, and areas of need. If the goal is to move the group toward deeper relationships and a deeper experience of God, then a structured agenda is the best way to achieve that goal.

6. **Fearless Foursomes:** Dividing your small group into foursomes during the Bible study can be a good idea. Here are some advantages and disadvantages:

   **Advantages:** Many people will feel less threatened in a group of four. It is easier to talk in front of four people instead of 12+ people. Also, there is simply not enough time in this portion of the meeting to allow everyone to talk.

   **Disadvantages:** It can take longer to get to know everyone if you only get to be in a foursome with everyone after several meetings. Also, you might have to retell your story during the prayer time if you already shared the details with your foursome. Each foursome might want to summarize what each person said once the group regathers.

Take a moment looking at the different Serendipity small group materials. Choose one session from each of the sample booklets in your kit and see if you can identify:

❏ Ice-Breaker
❏ Gradual disclosure
❏ Open-ended, right-brain questions
❏ Multiple choice options
❏ Tight agenda
❏ Heart-Warmer

The diagram below shows how you can use small group material and move your groups from simple, "getting acquainted" groups, all the way to service and personal ministry inventories!

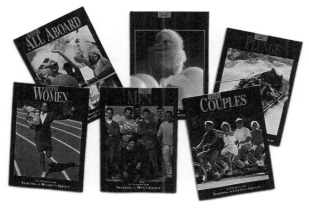

**Stage 1: Kick Off Groups**
Group: Men's Group, Women's Group, Couple's
   group, etc.
Material: Serendipity's 101 Series
Features: Non-threatening, level playing field to share
   your history
Covenant: 6 weeks
Need met: Friendship and belonging

**Stage 2: On-Going and Special Interest Groups**
Group: Stress, Parenting, Divorce Recovery,
   Single Again
Material: Serendipity's "201 Series"
Features: Encourages group empathy and affinity
   in a place of healing
Covenant: 12 weeks
Need met: Major felt need

**Stage 3: Bible Study Groups**
Group: Couples, Men, Women, Mixed, etc.
Material: Serendipity's "301 Series"
Features: Inductive study with two different tracks
Covenant: 12 weeks
Need met: Biblical guidance

**Stage 4: Graduation and Preparation for Releasing**
Group: Couples, Men, Women, Mixed, etc.
Material: Serendipity's "401 Series"
Features: Helps group say goodbye while
   assessing strengths and interests
Covenant: 6 weeks
Need met: Giving back to God

**401**
Coming
in 1995

# How Does a Group Choose a Ministry Project?

Every small group needs to remain balanced. By devoting themselves to a ministry project, a small group can remain balanced **and** take advantage of the synergy a small group provides.

Your small group director will help you choose a ministry project for your group. Use the space below to take notes regarding ministry projects in your small group program.

# *Self-Quiz #3*

**Bible Study:** The Bible contains a wealth of information about small groups.

The early church adopted the same "corporate-ness" of Old Testament Judaism and Jesus' group of disciples. It is in the book of Acts that we read of the first recorded instances of the early church meeting in homes (Acts 2:46; 5:42; 8:3; 20:20-21). The book of Acts also stresses the importance of in-house intimacy and large-group worship: "Day after day, in the temple courts and house to house, they never stopped teaching and proclaiming the good news that Jesus is the Christ" (5:42). Acts 2:42-47 elaborates on this twofold approach to ministry in the early church: (1) Corporate worship together, (2) Caring in homes.

*"They devoted themselves to the apostles' teaching and to the fellowship, to the breaking of bread and to prayer. Everyone was filled with awe, and many wonders and miraculous signs were done by the apostles. All the believers were together and had everything in common. Selling their possessions and goods, they gave to anyone as he had need. Every day they continued to meet together in the temple courts. They broke bread in their homes and ate together with glad and sincere hearts, praising God and enjoying the favor of all the people. And the Lord added to their number daily those who were being saved."*

List some of the characteristics of the early church included in this passage:

**Reflection:** These questions give you a chance to reflect back on what you learned in Session 3. You might be asked to share your answers at the next session.

1. The idea of gradually moving a group towards a time of trust and openness is very important for a successful small group agenda. Can you think of a time when you were expected to "open up" but did not feel ready or safe? What was it like?

2. Think of the different groups you have been a part of (school classes, work teams, Sunday school classes, families, etc.). Make a list of these groups. Next to each group write down the level of communication the group typically experienced:

3. Can you think of a time when you were ready and eager to tell a group of people how you were feeling or what God was doing in your life, only to discover they were not interested? What was it like?

4. In what ways would a group be hindered if they tried to use "personal Bible study" material instead of material written for a small group?

5. How is a Christian support group different than a secular support group?

**Preparation:** Get ready for Session 4 by answering the following questions:

1. What type of small group would you like to lead? What type of group would you prefer **not** to lead?

2. How do you handle conflict in your relationships?

3. If you lead a small group, how will you know if you are doing a good job?

**Prayer:** Before your next meeting, pray about the following. . .

A small group should be a place where people can "be themselves," and talk openly about their lives. Many times this can be very emotional and powerful. Pray that God will help you prepare yourself to create a safe, accepting atmosphere as a small group leader.

# Session 4

In Session 4 we will discuss. . .

- **What is a healthy small group?**. . . . . . . . . . . . . . . . . . . . . . . . . . . . . . . . . . . 36

- **What if there is a problem?**. . . . . . . . . . . . . . . . . . . . . . . . . . . . . . . . . . . . .37

- **Can small groups have fun, too?**. . . . . . . . . . . . . . . . . . . . . . . . . . . . . . .39

- **Self-quiz #4**. . . . . . . . . . . . . . . . . . . . . . . . . . . . . . . . . . . . . . . . . . . . . . . .40

# *What Is a Healthy Small Group?*

What does a healthy small group look like? This list is adapted from one developed by Roberta Hestenes (*Growing the Church Through Small Groups,* 1985). What are the qualities of a healthy group in your small group program?

- ❑ **A clear purpose:** The group needs to have a shared understanding of the group's purpose and the how to accomplish it. The best way to create a purpose is to get two or three people together who have a similar purpose and have them invite others to join with them.

- ❑ **Helpful leaders:** We will look at this closely in the last training session, but a helpful leader is basically one that is prayerful, prepared, and active in the life of the group. Good leadership does not just happen. People need to be trained and supported.

- ❑ **Identification of new leaders:** No small group should be dependent on one or two leaders. A small group is the ideal place to recognize people's gifts and encourage them to find their own special place of leadership.

- ❑ **Worthwhile content:** The content of the discussion needs to be both interesting and relevant to the group's purposes. We recommend using Serendipity materials. If you choose other small group materials, make sure they are designed not only to do Bible study, but also include group building.

- ❑ **Growing trust and caring:** One of the goals in any small group is learning to love one another. Over a period of weeks and months, self-disclosure should grow as the group is guided in that direction. If conflict arises along the way, don't smother it. Deal with it as a group. Correctly handled, it will deepen the trust and care of members.

- ❑ **Compassion for those without Christ:** By keeping an empty chair as a reminder of those people who need the group, and constantly praying for and seeking people who can be brought into the group, a small group develops a healthy sense of lifestyle evangelism.

- ❑ **Opportunities for service:** A healthy feature of a small group is the ability to stretch outside themselves and minister to others in Jesus' name.

- ❑ **Centered in Jesus Christ:** One important reminder about Christian small groups. We are called to follow Jesus and His purposes in small groups. If a small group loses touch with why it is meeting, bring it back to the purpose as followers of Jesus. In most groups, this will also mean a time for prayer. Be sure to leave adequate time for prayer requests and caring.

- ❑ **A good beginning:** A healthy small group realizes the importance of getting off to a good start. This involves prayerful planning, careful preparation and a warm awareness of each member.

# What If There Is a Problem?

Consider the following situations and problems that might occur in a small group meeting. Use the space to make notes about what **you** would do if you were the leader of the group in question.

### Jethro

*It seems that every time Jethro Yakovich has a thought, he shares it with the group. Jethro is notorious for dominating the conversation and taking up more than his share of the time. Other group members do not get a chance to talk. People are getting restless and thinking about quitting the group. What do you do without hurting Jethro's feelings or making the group feel like they are not free to talk?*

### Floyd

*Floyd Fist has kept very quiet during the first few weeks of the support group for "Parents of Teenagers." However, when the topic turns to discipline, Floyd perks up. He quietly mentions that he sometimes "has to straighten out" his children, who are 14- and 16-year old boys. When the leader says, "What do you mean, Floyd?" he admits that he sometimes uses physical force, "but only when they really provoke me." Several other members gasp, and the rest silently shake their heads. What should the group leader do?*

### Carolyn

*The Couples Group, in their second year, has been discussing communication when Carolyn starts talking about communication problems in her marriage. She blurts out that she once had an affair with a man with whom she could really communicate. An awkward silence follows. What should the leader do? What would you do if her husband was not present! What if he was?*

### Myron

*Myron means well, he's just over enthusiastic. He's only been a believer for a few months, and joining the study group seemed like a good idea. Myron, however, is getting frustrated with his Bible knowledge. He can't seem to learn fast enough to keep up. Last night, the leader asked, "Who was responsible for taking the gospel to the Roman world?" "Noah!" Myron says loudly. Some of the group members start to giggle. What should the leader do?*

### Betty

*The word has gotten back to the "Dysfunctional Family Recovery Group" that Betty Babbler has been talking to other people about the group. She has even told some of the stories, with names, that other group members have told. As this news is told in the group, people begin to feel angry. And they were wondering why their stories were showing up on the prayer list in the church newsletter. What should the leader do?*

### Judy and Bart

*The Discipleship Group has been talking about angels. Bart, the group leader, tells the group that an infinite number of angels can stand on the head of a pin and anyone who does not believe this is condemned to hell. Judy disagrees. She says that Archangels are different and Bart is a theological nitwit. The more she talks the angrier she gets. Bart is getting angry too. Before you know it, the group has taken sides on this issue and are arguing full force. The leader steps in and whistles loudly. Silence follows, but everyone is still riled up. What should the leader do next?*

Have you ever been in any of these situations in a small group? What happened? What did the leader do? Was a proper solution found?

# Can Small Groups Have Fun, Too?

**Having Fun!**

Some people call it fellowship. The point is, small groups need to know that it is O.K. to have fun together. Fun and fellowship adds a "real-life" component to a group and helps them become good friends. The Guacamole Group in Austin, Texas, has quarterly "Game night," an annual Inner-tube trip down the Guadalupe River, and an occasional retreat!

Regular fellowship reinforces the idea of being a group between meetings. Here are some ideas for making contact with each other when the group is not in their meeting:

- Use the **telephone.** Call someone and ask them how they can be prayed for. If someone at the meeting was silent, or ignored or even absent, call them and offer a word of encouragement.

- Take another group member **out to lunch** during the week, just for the fun of it.

- **Sit together** in church, and then go to lunch together, with your families, after church.

- **Write a note** of appreciation to a group member who has inspired you or a group member that needs encouragement.

- Plan a fun **group activity** together, bring the family! Bowling, picnic, movie, circus, concert, swimming, Christmas caroling, hayride, taffy pull, progressive dinner, ice cream social, wienie roast. . . the possibilities are endless.

- Some small groups schedule **fun nights.** The group gets together for games, like Pictionary, charades, Outburst, Twister (!), or the Newlywed Game for couples groups.

- Take a **road trip!** This is a great way for a group to "connect." A group can go to an area hotel for a weekend and have their own retreat, or the group can go out of town, stay in a Bed-and-Breakfast and see the sights! A group could even plan a camping trip together!

Remember: Social events are a great way to reach out to new group members.

# Self-Quiz #4

 **Bible Study:** The Bible contains a wealth of information about small groups.

The Apostle Paul was the consummate churchman. Paul started dozens of churches in the Greco-Roman world, and almost all of them met in homes (Romans 16:10,15; 1 Corinthians 1:11,16; 16:20; Philippians 4:22; Colossians 4:15; Philemon 2). The early church was deeply relational and intimate, a feature many churches have lost.

The New Testament epistles were letters written to people who lived out their Christianity in small groups. Most of the time, these groups met in homes. Small groups were a basic part of the Christian life when the New Testament was written. Many times we read these letters as if they were written to individuals, when they were actually written to groups.

The relationships described in the New Testament are exciting and wonderful, and they were meant to happen in the small group setting. Consider the following verses and imagine what these relationships might have been like:

1. **Everyone contributes something**. "But to each one the manifestation of the Spirit is given for the common good" (1 Cor. 12:7). Later in the same epistle we read: "When you come together, each one has a psalm, a lesson, a revelation, a tongue, or an interpretation. All of these must be done for the strengthening of the church" (14:26).

   The small group is the ideal place for "each one" to share their relationship with God. What do you think happens among a group of people when each person has the chance to share like this?

2. **Sympathetic Behavior.** "If one part suffers, every part suffers with it; if one part is honored, every part rejoices with it" (I Cor. 12:26).

   What difference would it make in someone's life if they were able to share their joys and grief with other church members?

3. **Family Language:** The New Testament writers use a great variety of family terms to describe the church and church relationships. Consider these terms: *brother, sister, orphan, children, father, household, servant, household slave, house, nanny, tutor, wet-nurse, etc.*

   Why would the epistle writers use this kind of language? What would happen if a group of church members took on the qualities that these terms imply?

**3. Group Prayer:** In the epistles, which were written to house churches and even read aloud during their meetings, prayer is mentioned frequently. (Unfortunately, we do not read these references to prayer as group instructions, but as private or individual instructions.)

What happens to a group when they share their prayer requests with one another, and then pray for one another?

**Reflection:** These questions give you a chance to reflect back on what you learned in Session 4. You might be asked to share your answers at the next session.

1. Consider the qualities of a healthy small group. Can you think of any other qualities of a small group which will help you determine whether or not the groups in your program are healthy?

2. How did you feel as you read about the various problems that might occur in a small group?

**Preparation:** Get ready for Session 5 by answering the following questions:

1. Have you ever been part of a group that seemed to "mature" over time? What happened? What was the group like when it started? What was it like as it matured?

2. Have you ever been the "new person" at a small group or a class? What was it like?

3. Are the church programs you are currently a part of actively trying to find new members or participants?

**Prayer:** Before your next meeting, pray about the following. . .

An important component of a healthy group is remaining "Christ-centered." What are you doing in your life to walk with Christ each day? Pray that your relationship with Christ will be vital and alive in a way that will help assure that your small group is "Christ-centered."

# Session 5

**In Session #5, we will discuss. . .**

- Can a small group "grow up"?. . . . . . . . . . . . . . . . . . . . . . . . . . . . . . . . . 43
- How long does community take?. . . . . . . . . . . . . . . . . . . . . . . . . . . . . . . 44
- When can a small group leader "step back"?. . . . . . . . . . . . . . . . . . . . . 45
- Should groups always be open to new people?. . . . . . . . . . . . . . . . . 46
- What is our strategy for multiplying groups?. . . . . . . . . . . . . . . . . . . . 48
- Self-quiz #5. . . . . . . . . . . . . . . . . . . . . . . . . . . . . . . . . . . . . . . . . . . . . . . 49

# Can a Small Group "Grow Up"?

## What is a Lifecycle?

Like any living organism, a small group has a lifecycle. In its own way, the lifecycle of groups is as beautiful to behold as the lifecycle of people and their families.

Let's take a look at the stages of a small group. These stages can be seen in groups that stay together for at least several months.

**Stage 1:** _____ (1st month)

The initial idea of beginning a group is conceived and the first meetings are held. A group is highly dependent upon the leader in this stage and you might find members raising their hands when they want to speak. The group is eager, but not sure what to expect. The excitement of making new friends and the euphoria of becoming close to people begins to emerge.

**Stage 2:** _____ (2nd-3rd month)

The group begins to form its own identity and personality. Control of the group is established at this point. A meeting format evolves as the group relies on the leader for guidance. Initial relationship-building and pattern-setting begins. It is a challenge for the leader to begin to let the group assert their own group personality.

**Stage 3:** _____ (3rd-5th month)

A time of questioning—a few members may even begin to complain about group meetings or activities. The group is deciding how close they will come to one another, how much they will trust each other. Leaders need to allow questioning and accept the need for adjustments. Recognize that some conflict is a necessary part of building close relationships.

**Stage 4:** _____ (5th to 18th month)

The group has taken on a life and energy of its own—it is accomplishing the purpose for which it was formed. Leaders need to maintain the excitement by taking advantage of the closeness the group has developed. This is the time of joy, laughter, as the group is prepared to fulfill their group covenant with great enthusiasm.

**Stage 5:** _____ (18th month +)

At this stage the group will either redefine its purpose and gain new energy or it will lose members, interest and eventually die. The task of the leader is to give the group a new vision and/or recognize that the group needs to die gracefully. Helping the group, or individual members, find their next "passion" is an important task for the leader during this stage.

# How Long Does Community Take?

**The Baseball Diamond**
Anyone who's been around Serendipity at all has probably heard of the baseball diamond. The strategy explains how a small group, over time, can achieve *koinonia,* or *community.* This is a tried and true method for building a foundation for group intimacy in as little as six weeks. *Serendipity* uses this method and it is built into their "kick-off" material (101 Series). A close familiarity with this strategy can help build a group regardless of the situation or material.

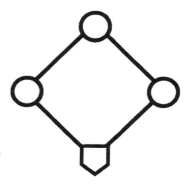

**First Base: History Giving.** The greatest gift you can give your group is the gift of yourself. First base is called history giving because you share your story with the rest of the group. In some instances, this will be a simple "get acquainted" time. On other occasions, you will "unpack your baggage," take off your coat, and reveal a milestone in your story.

First base is the place you share your spiritual journey:

- YOUR PAST:       Roots and memories, significant others
- YOUR PRESENT:    Where you are right now in your spiritual pilgrimage
- YOUR FUTURE:     Where you want to be. Your hopes and dreams. Your calling from God

**Second Base: Affirmation.** Second base is responding to the person who shared their trip around first base. Second base creates a relationship between people. But the relationship is more than "feedback" or proper listening skills. Second base is a place of unconditional acceptance, a total affirmation of the person and their story.

Second base says, "Thanks for sharing. . . I appreciate what you have been through. . . Your story is a real gift to me because. . ." Every group must learn how to do this with each other.

**Third Base: Goal Setting.** Sharing and affirmation form relationships. Relationships become bonded into a group by risking and venturing out into uncharted waters. Third base is sharing on a deeper level: "Where do you need to grow. . .?" "Where is God calling you. . .?" "What seems to be keeping you from this change in your life. . ." Third base is the place where the Holy Spirit bonds people together.

**Home Plate: Koinonia.** Duke Ellington was once asked to define rhythm. He responded, "If you got it, you don't need no definition. If you ain't got it, no definition is gonna help." Koinonia, like rhythm, defies definition. Some say it is community, a symphony, a bonding.

# *When Can a Small Group Leader "Step Back"?*

### The Flying Wedge

We've already considered the 3-legged stool. We learned that there are three essential elements in a healthy group. Now we will learn how to shuffle these three elements within a meeting depending on where that group is in its lifecycle.

Imagine a group that has agreed to meet from September to May, just like the school year. The picture below illustrates the change in the elements of the meeting over that nine month period. During the first stage, the group needs to devote most of their time on group-building. Then, after the group has become a group, you can shift the formula to allow more time for Bible study and ministry. And by the end of the year, when the covenant begins to wind down, the group can end their time together and say good-bye with reflection and celebration activities.

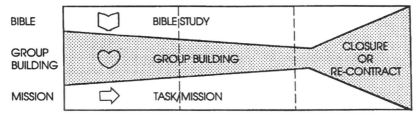

Now look at the lifecycle of a group more closely.

• In the Birth period, the purpose is to become a group
• In the Growth period, the purpose is to grow in scripture and spiritual formation
• In the Release period, the purpose is to get ready to graduate and parent new groups

In each period, the approach to Bible study varies. For instance, in the Birth period, the Bible study approach is to launch the playing field (101).

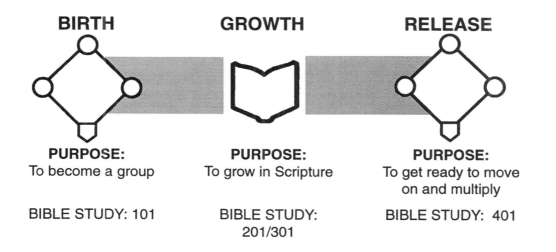

| **BIRTH** | **GROWTH** | **RELEASE** |
|---|---|---|
| **PURPOSE:** | **PURPOSE:** | **PURPOSE:** |
| To become a group | To grow in Scripture | To get ready to move on and multiply |
| BIBLE STUDY: 101 | BIBLE STUDY: 201/301 | BIBLE STUDY: 401 |

# Should Groups Always Be Open to New People?

There are several important factors to consider in the discussion of whether or not groups should be open to new members. This is an important issue because it is common for groups to hesitate to reach out because their group has become "comfortable."

**The Rolling Covenant**
We've already discussed the idea of the group covenant. Rolling covenants are covenants which are periodically re-negotiated or "rolled over." In the course of negotiating these covenants, a time-period is set for the duration of the covenants (six weeks or twelve weeks, for example). At the end of the period the covenants can be evaluated and either re-affirmed or re-negotiated.

Suppose the "Overweight Non-smoking Men Who Love to Shop" Group got started and agreed to meet for six weeks so they could get to know each other. After six weeks, they decided to renegotiate their covenant for an additional 12 weeks, remaining open to new members for the first half of this covenant, and closed to new members for the second six weeks.

Rolling covenants help settle the issue of whether groups should be open or closed to new members. For example, a rolling covenant may allow the group to be open during the first half of the covenant, but closed during the second half. A rolling covenant recognizes the need for outreach, but also acknowledges that community-building should not be interrupted too frequently by the introduction of new members. The rolling covenant also gives people a chance to leave the group gracefully, between covenants.

| ROLLING COVENANTS | | |
|---|---|---|
| FIRST COVENANT | RE-COVENANT | RE-COVENANT |
| OPEN    CLOSED<br>First    Second<br>Half    Half | OPEN    CLOSED<br>First    Second<br>Half    Half | OPEN    CLOSED<br>First    Second<br>Half    Half |

## The Empty Chair

The empty chair makes the group notice someone who is not there. It is a visual cue to the group that there are people out there who desperately need what the group has to offer. Pull an empty chair in the group in the closing prayer time and consciously pray that God will fill the chair with the person that he wants to come to the next meeting. The empty chair will be a constant reminder that your group is "open" to others.

## Welcoming New Members

When someone new joins a group, it is important that they feel as comfortable with the group as the rest of the members. This is especially true if the rest of the group has already been meeting together. Simply being aware of how a new person might feel is the first step toward making them feel at home. The group should strive together to make the person feel welcome. Here are some suggestions which will facilitate this process:

**First,** as the "organizer" of a small group, the leader would be the contact person for new group members. Therefore, the leader can do a great deal **introducing** the new person to the group. That can best be done by the leader informally interviewing the new person in the presence of the group, or telling the group the basic information about the new person, such as their name and how they found out about the group.

Some small group programs ask potential members to fill out an information sheet. These questionnaires avoid overly-intrusive questions, and they are designed to help a group leader get basic information about a potential member. With this information in hand, the leader knows who is coming and how to introduce them properly.

**Second,** the new member will need to be told about the **Group Covenant.** This will help the new person get "up to speed" with the direction the group is headed.

**Third,** the new member will probably need to be given about ten minutes when the entire group is together to **tell their story.** This can be done in a variety of ways, but care must be taken not to put the new person "on the spot" and make them feel too uncomfortable. It might be a good idea to let everyone else in the group tell a little bit about themselves first. Don't forget that it will take a new group member some time to settle into the familiarity and intimacy that the rest of the group has already developed.

**Fourth,** the group might consider waiting to bring new members into the group when they are **renegotiating their covenant.** This depends how far along the group is in their covenant period when news of a new member is shared.

**Fifth,** the group should be reminded that the newcomer does not **have to join the group,** even after they have visited the group. If the person does not decide to join the group, the other members should not be overly concerned, it was probably not a good match.

# What Is Our Strategy for Multiplying Groups?

Forming new groups from existing ones is a powerful way to expand a wonderful ministry and bring more people to Christ. Use the space below to make notes about the strategy for multiplying groups at your church:

# Self-Quiz #5

 **Bible Study:** The Bible contains a wealth of information about small groups.

<u>One Another!</u> This short phrase has implications for the church that are powerful. When you read the New Testament Epistles, you will find "one another" phrases 59 times. Each occurrence of this phrase indicates relationships which should be going on among church members. Of course, the small group is a tremendous place for these types of relationships to occur. As you read these phrases, write down **your ideas** about how these "one anothers" can happen in a small group:

**"Care for one another. . ."** 1 Corinthians 12:25

**"Offer hospitality to one another. . ."** 1 Peter 4:9

**"Accept one another. . ."** Romans 15:7

**"Honor one another above yourselves. . ."** Romans 12:10

**"Bear one another's burdens. . ."** Galatians 6:2

**"Be at peace with one another. . ."** Mark 9:50

**"Confess to one another. . ."** James 5:16

**"Build up one another. . ."** 1 Thessalonians 5:11

**"Forgive one another. . ."** Ephesians 4:32

**"Be kind and compassionate to one another. . ."** Ephesians 4:32

**"Serve one another. . ."** 1 Peter 4:10

**"Offer hospitality to one another. . ."** 1 Peter 4:9

**"Encourage one another. . ."** 1 Thessalonians 5:11

**"Live in harmony with one another. . ."** 1 Peter 4:8

**"Love one another. . ."** 1 John 4:11

**"Teach one another. . ."** Colossians 3:16

**" Be devoted to one another. . ."** Romans 12:10

**"Pray for one another. . ."** James 5:16

 **Reflection:** These questions give you a chance to reflect back on what you learned in Session 5. You might be asked to share your answers at the next session.

1. Have you ever experienced *koinonia?* What was it like?

2. Do you think it will be easy or difficult to keep a group open to new members? Why?

3. Do you think it will be easy or difficult to form a new group out of an existing one—even if it means taking away some group members to form the new group? Why?

 **Preparation:** Get ready for Session 6 by answering the following questions.

1. Do you remember the last time you started a new small group or Sunday School class? How did you feel? Were you prepared?

2. Have you ever been a part of a relationship that had a bad ending? What happened? How could the bad ending have been avoided?

3. Have you ever volunteered for a church or ministry position only to feel abandoned by the people who were supposed to watch over you? What happened? How did it feel?

 **Prayer:** Before your next meeting, pray about the following. . .

As the small group leader training winds down, pray for the success of your small group program. Pray for your small group director, that he/she will be submissive to God in the leadership of this program. Pray for your fellow small group leaders. Besides praying for the specific needs in their lives, pray that God will guide them and bless them in a special way as they begin this new opportunity to serve Him.

# Session ⑥

**This is our last session. Our topics for Session #6 include. . .**

• **What kind of people join a small group?**. . . . . . . . . . . . . . . . . . . . . . . . . . . . . . 52

• **How do I start a group?**. . . . . . . . . . . . . . . . . . . . . . . . . . . . . . . . . . . . . . . 53

• **How does a small group end?**. . . . . . . . . . . . . . . . . . . . . . . . . . . . . . . . . . . .55

• **What is on our small group calendar?**. . . . . . . . . . . . . . . . . . . . . . . . . . . . . . 57

• **Where can a leader get support?**. . . . . . . . . . . . . . . . . . . . . . . . . . . . . . . . . 58

• **Self-quiz #6.**. . . . . . . . . . . . . . . . . . . . . . . . . . . . . . . . . . . . . . . . . . . . 60

# What Kind of People Join a Small Group?

Here are 11 true-false questions that will help you identify your potential group members. This list is adapted from Neal McBride's *How to Lead Small Groups* (pp. 57-58). These are only generalizations, but they might help you understand your group members better:

**true  false**

❏  ❏  People join groups to satisfy an individual need. Their primary motivation is usually self-centered.

❏  ❏  A person will join **or** remain in a small group if he finds the group's goals and activities attractive and rewarding.

❏  ❏  People prefer to participate in a group where other members are similar in age, attractiveness, attitudes, personality, economic status, perceived ability, and needs. Homogenous groups like this are easier to form, but groups with diverse members (ages, lifestyle, gender, race) perform more effectively.

❏  ❏  Total overall participation in a small group increases with increasing group size. The smaller the group, the less its individual members participate.

❏  ❏  Group members usually evaluate larger groups more positively than smaller ones.

❏  ❏  The smaller the group, the greater the feasibility of shared leadership. Increasing group size increases the probability of a focused leader rather than shared leadership.

❏  ❏  The physical setting where the group meets does not affect the members attitudes, actions, and the group process. The meeting place has very little impact on members' participation in the group.

❏  ❏  Individual group members' level of social and psychological adjustment has no affect on the group process.

❏  ❏  How long a group member has been a Christian has a significant impact on the success of the group process.

❏  ❏  Members are more highly motivated and perform more efficiently when the group possesses clear goals and an understanding of what must be done to accomplish the goals. Knowing why and how the group exists stimulates higher levels of participation.

❏  ❏  Shared ownership of specific goals builds positive interaction in the group.

# *How Do I Start a Group?*

"You only get one beginning, so you better make it a good one." This saying is especially true for small groups. As a small group leader, you need to know how to start a small group.

**Getting Ready to Start a Small Group**
You will not be expected to start a group until **you** are ready. Here is a list of steps each group leader needs to complete before they actually start a group.

**First,** pray, pray, pray. Each small group leader needs to pray intently about leading a group, knowing that God cares very much about their desire to serve Him.

**Second,** each small group leader should review any of the material from the training sessions that they are not familiar with. It is important that each group leader has a working knowledge of the training material.

**Third,** plan a meeting with the small group director. This meeting will address several issues. How do you feel about leading a group right now? When is a good time for you to begin leading a group? What kind of group would you like to lead? Which evenings would you be able to lead your group?

**Fourth,** each small group leader needs an assistant or apprentice leader. This will give the new leader more confidence, and will prepare someone to lead the group when it's time to multiply. The new leader will also need a host or hostess. Hopefully, one of the group members will offer their home for the group meeting.

**Fifth,** the group leader and apprentice leader need to begin putting together a prospect list. Potential group members might be friends, acquaintances, people at church, neighbors or co-workers. Where prospective group members come from depends greatly on the type of group which is being offered. This list of potential members might be supplemented by the small group director (names gathered from needs assessment surveys, for example).

**Sixth,** group leaders should begin contacting potential group members. Usually an informal telephone call is sufficient. This will help the leader know a little bit about each person which is helpful when introducing new group members to one another. A reminder card sent to potential group members is a good idea. Also, some churches do not publicize the location of certain groups, in order to protect the anonymity of group members. In this case, potential group members need to be told where the group will meet.

**Seventh,** the group leader will need recommendations for the material to use in their meetings. Most groups can get off to a great start with booklets from Serendipity's "101 Series," which are specifically designed to help groups get off on the right foot.

## Your First Meeting

Being ready for your first meeting is important, but not difficult. The following steps should be completed before your first meeting:

- Make sure you have an **accurate list** of who will be attending your first meeting. As people call, remember the pertinent information about them. This way you will know how many people will show up and what their names are.

- The leader should show up early and go over with the **host and/or hostess** the details of the group. Discuss the Host/Hostess job description (this is available from your small group director). Make sure the meeting area is set up properly and the leader can make eye contact with each group member. If the leader plans on using foursomes during the meeting, this space should be identified. The leader also needs to make sure the meeting area is free from distractions. Refreshments are a good idea for the first meeting.

- There must be **enough booklets.** It is usually a good idea for the group members to buy their own materials. This way they are less likely to lose them and they have made a small investment in the group. **Pencils** might also be a good idea. Also, **name tags** would be helpful during the first few meetings. Having a few extra **Bibles** would also be a good idea.

- The leader needs to be prepared to **lead the meeting.** Does the leader have a meeting agenda? Has the leader familiarized himself with the Ice-Breaker, the Bible study, and the Heart-Warmer? If the group is going to discuss the **group covenant,** does everyone have a copy? Each leader needs to know that their new group members will feel most comfortable if the first few meetings are well planned.

- The leader needs to be prepared to **greet** everyone and introduce everyone in your group. In addition to the Ice-Breaker in the material you are using, you may wish to go around and ask everyone to say their name, occupation, and family information.

- The leader also needs to make sure **childcare** arrangements have been made and everyone is aware of these arrangements.

- **After the meeting,** the leader should contact each person and tell them they were glad to attend the meeting.

- The leader needs to explain why there is an **empty chair** sitting in the circle. Reminding the group that there are other people who need what the group has to offer should begin early.

# *How Does a Small Group End?*

No small group was meant to last forever. Here is a list of reasons why small groups end:

**The stated length of time expires.** This is an ideal reason for a group disbanding, especially those groups that began with a clearly defined time span included in the group covenant.

**The task is accomplished.** Rarely is the "task" completed in Relationship Groups or Need-based Groups. The ending of content- or task-oriented groups, on the other hand, makes sense when the task is done.

**The group explodes in conflict.** When this happens it is bad news. If conflict does occur, it happens fairly early in the life of the group.

**A covenant has not been secured.** Lacking group norms, the attendance and behavior of the group members disintegrates to the point where all agree that continuing is fruitless.

**A conscious decision is made to terminate.** This is a logical choice on the part of group members. Schedule conflicts, members moving out of town, the desire to try something new, or reformation of the group are all examples of reasons why groups might choose to terminate.

**Group leadership is not sufficient or properly matched to the agenda of the group.** This is hard on us as leaders. Yet, at times, we may be in over our heads. Task-, need-, and content-oriented groups are susceptible to leadership failure. Process-oriented groups are as well, but because of their very nature, they tend to be more forgiving of improperly designated leaders.

**The group multiplies to form two new groups.** Some churches multiply groups when they reach a certain size and form new groups. This works well in a limited number of situations.

**Poor administration.** Problems with time, place, frequency, scheduling causes members to give up and not participate. These problems are fairly easy to avoid.

**Members are not compatible.** Whether by choice or conflict, sometimes group members do not get along well. This might be because of personality conflicts, or simply too great a variety in age and experience.

55

**How to End a Small Group Gracefully**

Ending a small group, or even creating a new covenant can be a difficult experience. Closing a group needs to be done carefully. The friendships built in a small group can be the most meaningful relationships many people have. There are certain things a small group leader should be aware of when closing a group. Remember that the beginning of a group and the end of a group are the most critical times for the leader to take an active role.

**First,** make sure the group is prepared for the last meeting before it arrives. The group leader should mention that the last meeting is coming several weeks in advance. For best results, use material specifically written for groups that are ending, such as Serendipity's "401 Series." The group members need plenty of time to prepare themselves for the last meeting.

**Second,** be flexible regarding the format of your last meeting. Don't feel like you have to follow the regular agenda during that last meeting. The most important thing you can do is make sure everyone goes their separate ways with the greatest amount of comfort and confidence. Let the group spend some time evaluating their experience together in a positive way.

**Third,** end on a good note. Do some kind of exercise which involves affirmation. Let everyone say something good about someone else, or let everyone share how the group has been helpful for them. Give everyone the chance to share their feelings for the group.

**Fourth,** try to plan an activity in the future when your group can get back together. Remind your group that the relationships they have built do not have to end, but they can continue to be friends and do things together. It might be good to plan a reunion meeting when everyone can be together again, perhaps a month later. Also, let the group members know about other opportunities to get involved in a small group.

**Fifth,** devote an extra amount of time to prayer. Let your group take advantage of what they have built together by making their last prayer time together as special as possible.

# What Is On Our Small Group Calendar?

Use this calendar to record what is going on in your small group program this year:

| January | February | March |
|---|---|---|
| April | May | June |
| July | August | September |
| October | November | December |

# Where Can a Leader Get Support?

As a small group leader, you have special needs. You are a minister, on the "front lines" of Christian service. As a valuable servant, your small group director has planned ways for you to be supported.

Use the space below to record how your small group director is going to help you find the support you need as a small group leader.

In order to help you, your small group director needs information from you. The form on the following page is an example of a form that you can use to give your small group director valuable information about your group.

# *Small Group Report Form*

Name of group: _____Date: _____

Leader's name: _____

Apprentice leader's name: _____

Host or hostess: _____

| Participant's name | Address | Phone | Code* |
|---|---|---|---|
| | | | |
| | | | |
| | | | |
| | | | |
| | | | |
| | | | |
| | | | |
| | | | |
| | | | |

* Mark "V" for visitors, "RV" for return visitors, "NC" for New Christian and "CM" for church member.

How often do you contact your group members between meetings?
    ❏ several times each week    ❏ weekly    ❏ twice a month    ❏ monthly

What day of the week does your group meet? When does your meeting start and end?

How much time are you spending on the following activities:
    _____ Ice-Breaker        _____ Discussing group business
    _____ Bible study        _____ Prayer time

What is your group's ministry project?

Is your group ready to multiply? Why or why not?

What efforts have you made to contact prospective group members?

On a scale of 1 (lousy) to 10 (terrific), rate your recent small group experience:_____

Why? On the back write your praises, concerns and prayer requests. . .

# *Self-Quiz #6*

Your next meeting will be with your small group director. In order to be prepared, answer the following questions.

**Bible Study:** You are probably familiar with the "Great Commission."

*"Then Jesus came to them and said, 'All authority in heaven and and earth has been given to me. Therefore go and make disciples of all nations, baptizing them in the name of the Father and of the Son and of the Holy Spirit, and teaching them to obey everything I have commanded you. And surely I will be with you always, to the very end of the age."*
Matthew 28:18-20

1. As a potential small group leader anticipating your first small group meeting, how does it feel to know that "all authority in heaven and earth" has been given to Jesus?

2. What does it mean to you when Jesus says, "And surely I will be with you always. . ."?

3. Do you feel equipped to take your leadership skills into the world in Jesus' name? Why or why not?

**Reflection:** These questions give you a chance to reflect back on what you learned in Session 6. You might be asked to share your answers at the next session.

1. On the line below, mark how comfortable you feel with starting a new group:

_____

scared silly     full of doubts     kinda ready     fired up!

2. Have you ever been a part of a small group that ended? What happened?

3. Do you think you learned enough to start a small group? Are there other things about leading a small group you wish you knew?

4. Do you feel good about the support you will get as a small group leader?

**Preparation:**

1. What are your goals for your small group? How many people do you want in your group?

How many groups do you want to "multiply" out of your group?

Do you want to bring people to faith in Christ?

Do you want to introduce outsiders to the church?

What other goals do you have for your small group?

2. In what ways do you see your small group benefitting the lives of the participants?

3. Who do you have in mind to be in your group? What is your plan for bringing them into your group?

4. What night of the week would you like to meet on?

Where will you meet?

What will you do on your first meeting?

5. Use the form on the following page to begin planning your first meeting.

### A Meeting Worksheet

A similar copy of this worksheet can be found in the section of your "Small Group Starter Kit" marked "Forms." This worksheet will help you plan for your first few meetings and help you feel less nervous. (This worksheet was adapted from one originally written by Roberta Hestenes.)

**People:** Who is coming? Why are they coming? What special needs does each person have? What are their prayer concerns? Have you prayed for your group?

**Arrangements:** What needs to be done to prepare for the time together? What arrangements need to be made about the room, seating, Bibles, refreshments, childcare, materials, etc.? Who is in charge of these arrangements?

**Relationships:** How will you help people to feel cared for and caring? What will you do to help build positive relationships among the members of the group? (Ice-Breakers, introductions, checking-in, name tags, Heart-Warmers, etc.)

**Study/Task:** What steps will you follow to accomplish the task or complete the study? List the questions you will use and estimate the time for each one.

**Prayer:** What are your goals for the prayer time? How much time? What kind of prayer? Who will pray and when?

**Time:** What time is available and how will you divide it up? Do you have a meeting format? What is your "real" starting time? Your firm closing time? How will you move from each segment of your meeting? Are you attempting too much? Too little? Have you asked anyone to take responsibility for various portions of the meeting?

6. What issues, needs or interests would you like to focus on in your group?

7. What types of people, in what kinds of situations, would be most interested in your group?

8. Based on your answers to these "Preparation" questions, write a description of your group. Write this description as though it will be used in a brochure or catalog describing small groups. Try and write a description about 75 words in length.

9. The "Small Group Application" on the following page can help you get basic information on your group members. This information will help you know in advance who is coming to your group, and it can also help you introduce new members more thoroughly. Make copies of this form and give them to your potential group members, or ask for copies from your small group director.

**Prayer:**
Write a prayer about your upcoming experience as a small group leader. You might want to include praising God for what you've learned about Him during the training. Or thanking God for the opportunity to serve Him. You might choose to confess those areas in your life which might obstruct your efforts to be a Christ-like small group leader. Also, you might wish to pray specifically for those people who need to be a part of your small group.

# *Small Group Application*

Please answer the following questions about yourself:

Name: _____

Address: _____

Home phone:_____ Work phone: _____

What is your marital status: _____

How long have you lived in the area? _____

Are you a member of our church?    ❑ yes    ❑ no    If so, how long have you been a member?


What activities have you been involved in at our church?


Have you been in a small group before? Explain your experience:


Why do you want to be in a small group?


How did you hear about small groups at our church?